Stone Fruit

(and other works)

Emma A Woodard

BookLeaf Publishing

India | USA | UK

Made with ❤ on the BookLeaf Publishing Platform

www.bookleafpub.in

www.bookleafpub.com

Dedication

To Divine and John Waters, for proving that filth is an art form.

Preface

Stone Fruit is delicate—soft, bruisable, and fleeting.

It started as a collection of moments—small marks I've carried with me, stories that softened over time but never really faded. I wrote this because I couldn't let go of them, because I believe there's something powerful in the things that don't last forever.

Stone Fruit doesn't follow a straight path. It's a reflection on loss, longing, and the messy in-between of holding on and letting go. Some pieces will feel like whispers, others like echoes of things you thought you'd forgotten.

I hope this book finds you at a time that feels right. Whether you find sweetness or sorrow in it, know that you're holding something I once kept close. Thank you for sharing this with me.

Acknowledgements

"In order to write poetry that isn't political, I must listen to the birds, and in order to listen to the birds; the warplanes must be silent"
- Marwan Makhoul

Free Palestine.

1. Stone Fruit (Peach Pits)

It's not every day that I willingly freefall
Or find myself choosing
Spontaneous danger and adrenaline
But you give me that hit
That rush
That reason that I stop and I blush
And I giggle so loud
We get looks in the crowd
I go to bed at night and I honestly feel colder
How could I rest against a pillow, not your shoulder

Love songs are making sense again
Old thoughts of euphoria
Before my body kept score
Of the whore (and prima donna)
Like a virgin, your Madonna
Haven't felt a string like this
Tied so tight
Kept so long

I keep scissors on my belt
It helps, I fear
Make me present
Get me here
But you take me higher

You're my peach flavored lips
Bad breath, morning kiss
6 shots of espresso
There's still time
But let's go

I want to dive
I want to fall
I can somersault or cartwheel or crawl

I'm not begging you to love me
I'm begging me to let you in.

2. Hallowed Halls

You begged me to pray, to kneel
within the quiet confines of my closet,
wailing among your congregation.
So I praised, sang, danced, and cried out,
seeking to hear the words
that would heal the masses.

When your Lord spoke to me
in His velvet psalms of peace,
I heard only the songs
of my lover, whispering my name.

As I awaken in his arms,
existing in his life,
my heart now understands,
as you understand your God:
Lord, how I love mine.

3. Tie Guy

Oh, you in white, with your tie undone,
A soldier of God with battles unwon.
You spoke of His plan with a voice so sure,
But our whispers turned holy into impure.

How could I resist your trembling hands,
Guided by faith, bound by commands?
We knelt by the bed—not to pray, but in sin,
And the line between wrong and love grew thin.

You kissed me like scripture you'd longed to recite,
Tearing commandments in the dark of the night.
We broke them all, tore them apart,
Surrendered our souls and the walls of our hearts.

Your name was a hymn, your breath my prayer,
But shame clung to us in the dim, fragile air.
You were His emissary, ordained and true,
Yet your lips preached a gospel meant only for two.

I burned as you touched me, alive in the flame,
Yet drowned in the weight of my sin and my name.
Heaven closed its gates; the stars turned away,
As we made love where we were meant to obey.

I was Eve in the garden, I was salt turned to stone,
And you were Adam, breaking vows of your own.
Your white shirt was stained by the shadow of us,
A vessel cracked by forbidden trust.

Still, you swore, between breaths, you'd pray,
That we'd both be forgiven, somehow, someday.
But what use are prayers for a sin so deep,
When even angels must turn and weep?

I know the sun will swallow this fire,

Burn every lie, every shameful desire.
But for now, I carry the weight of our fall,
The curse of a love that was never meant at all.

Oh, Elder, loosen the tie, release me, please.
I'm drowning in guilt; I'm brought to my knees.
Your hands, so divine, yet they held me in sin—
A battle with God no one could win.

And though I love you, I must let you go,
For neither of us can ever atone.
This is our wilderness, our error, our flame—
You were my passion, my sin, and my shame.

4. Roasting to Charr

Why did I board a train
threatening to break down?

I could see them falling,
inches away from the ground.

But in the 500 miles
between me and the next town,
turning around
felt like breaking down.

My pilot's license expired
when I took myself down—
to kill the spire
winding too far toward *Babel.*

We babble,
but bleed in our words,
searching for the things
we whisper into existence.

A fear of falling folly,
overcome simply
by a fear of losing:

Letting go too soon.
Not keeping hold.

Slipping from my fingers
to close the distance,
watching this train break down—

when I've been studying
to be an Engineer.

Just one of many conductors

in the orchestra they present me—
the train needing to see town,
and town,
and world around.

This train
will not
break down.

5. Implicity...

I always said I'd write while with whiskey courage
Who knew
Illicit and dangerous
Would give me the red badge

Little squares make up hits
And bricks
I'm willing to gasp for air in
That river Styx

A soft powdered sugar cloud
Fantasies I don't cry out loud
Am I high from pills?
Is it the weed chills?

I'm falling in love with her
She's me, to be sure
Uninhibited at night
My pain feels right

I'm not unaware
The ache is still there
But I'm on my cloud
And I'm found in the crowd

Creature comfort cocaine
Gets a misanthrope out in the rain.

6. When She Stopped Running

I've been touched for years
Yes in my mind
But my body is on guard

I'm not used to not being used
So how can I expect to be used to you
I've felt the hand of both boy and man
I've tussled the curls of the woman and girl

In 3 decades
In coffee, iced tea, and lemonade
In all of the times my rent wasn't paid
I have never had hands
That caressed my shoulders
And held my thighs
Like I was something to be scared of losing.

Not innocence
Not ignorance
Nor feigning indifference
But respect for the lines
And the whole experience

He is not a person
An experience
A scene
My first hit of the day
Bringing haze to the age
Of vacating my cage

Our names, combined
On the spine of my journal
Your hand, in mine
In line, for snow bubble

Listening to music
Were there even lyrics
Close your eyes while driving
"Don't you make me steer this"

No, don't give me the handle
Don't try to light my candle
Don't love me, I will scramble.

Darlin.

7. Leap Date

Within silent bonds of faith,
All at once I wonder—
Was God at all aware of me
When He sent the sparks to fly?

February 29th,
a day out of place, like us.
Something caught
in time's fleeting hands,
existing because time itself
got tired of being perfect.

Once, every four years,
we come alive
in the coldest storm
February has to offer—
a fleeting burn, a rare delight,
our love bright enough to make
the longest night forget its dark.

Whatever we were—
accident, mistake, heavenly blur
with the weight
of an entire conclave
taking ownership of our play.

Fourteen years of longing,
compressed into one day.
No more time for games—
we're shooting stars,
exploding
across a sky
that was never meant
to hold us.

My love

was just too big
for ordinary years.
Too loud, too messy,
too alive — ?

Bursting forth
with joy, with pain, with tears.

And for a moment,
I'm free—
free to be
everything
I ever hoped to be,
everything
I was told I couldn't be.

How wonderful to hope again.
To dream again.
But February always ends.

And when it does,
I'll forget you — because I have to.
Because stories like ours
aren't allowed
to linger.

Till the next leap year,
we'll say goodbye—
our love
frozen in February's sky,
waiting
for time
to make another mistake.

If there were a god
to hear me,
I'd ask for one more leap day.

To be free.
With you.

8. Neat.

Drowning, drowning, dizzy and downing
Whiskey whispers, secrets swell
In the amber glow of the fading day

I lose myself, I drift, I stray

Drowning in the depths of a love gone wrong
Each sip a verse in a bitter song

I'm lost in the haze, but I long to be free
From this tempest of love that's drowning me

Wine's dark embrace, my ship, my sail
With every drink, a tether unspun
I cradle the glass, a fragile chalice
Filled with dreams of a love undone

But I yearn for the dawn, the soft kiss of day
To break free from the chains that your love cast away
I gather the courage, piece by piece
To rise from the depths, to reclaim my peace

With gin-soaked nights and rum-laced sighs
I drown the echoes of your cruel lies
The world spins in circles, a carousel of shame
As I seek to escape from the venom of your name

No longer drowning, no longer pale
I'll craft my own tale and set my sail
The strength in my heart will shatter the chain
I'll toast to the freedom of breaking the pain

Drowning, drowning, but learning to swim
In a love that no longer feels so grim

9. Run To Her!

I begged for you,
I fought for you,
I moved every line I ever set, just to get to you.

I cried for you,
I worked for you,
I stayed, I healed, I held on for you.

I wore your dreams like a second skin,
Hiding my shadows under your light,
Walking carefully around the broken parts of me,
All in the name of something we called love.

I learned your laughter,
Traded my quiet for your noise,
Whispered promises in the dark,
While the stars above just blinked, watching.

I painted my world with your colors,
Shaped my soul to fit your gaze,
A stranger in my own skin,
Mirrored in the reflection of your eyes.

I twisted my truths,
Bent my own hopes,
Chasing some bright future that never felt real,
Only to watch it fade as the sun rose.

I buried my fears in your needs,
Turned my pain into something soft,
Like love could ever fix the cracks,
Like love could take what I gave without taking
everything.

I stood at the edge of who I used to be,
A map with holes,

Trying to find my way to your heart,
But losing the path that led me back to mine.

I gave up my joy,
Surrendered my dreams,
Woven together with the weight of maybes,
Stitched with uncertainty.

But where did that wild person go?
The one who couldn't be contained,
Now chained by your expectations,
Stuck in a love that felt like giving in, not growing.

And yet, I still beg for you,
I still fight for you,
Wondering if the love I wanted was ever really mine,
Or just something you needed me to believe was.

In those quiet moments,
In the spaces where silence speaks,
I wonder—

Should love really feel like this?

A storm that takes everything,
Or should it be the thing that holds me,
Loving me for the mess I am,
Not for who I could become,
But for who I already am.

10. Voluntary Interactions

My hair was long and thick and coarse.
It sat in braids.
It stayed restrained.
It stayed down and made itself small.

It was thinned.
It was straightened for length,
perfumed,
colored.
No—not that color!

There are wrong colors?
Iron out my kinks,
tear the knots from the source.
Never fix—
simply change,
and change,
and alter.

A half step closer with a small root job,
a touch-up.
Make me look better.
Make me look pretty.
Make me acceptable,
passable,
palatable.

Shape me, gel me down,
stay in the place you need me to be in.

I wish I knew how I let it all get so long.
I know, I know—
I did it wrong.

Again, it's a cut,
a prod,

a dye,
a curl—
not those curls—soft waves!
Whiter brighter curls.

Strip the dull locks to bring the light,
wear colors to tint the water in your eyes.

The green is not yours.
That brown and tan not either.

Be whiter.
Be brighter.
Be straighter.
Be nicer.
Be more ladylike.

Speak when spoken to;
let social graces bury your screams for comfort.

11. Judgment of the Daughter of Gibeah

All the tilled and tender soil
hidden within the secret garden
of my mind's palace—
a gust of your breath scatters it.
The plains stretch barren now,
dust covering spaces where life once grew.

Tell me—is it love for you too?
Please, love, I offer my trust—
but let me know if all I am is lust.

Long are my years, heavy the weight
of what I was taught to uphold:
The Majesty of the Minx,
The Modesty of Mother.
Little maiden trustee, trusting,
taught to bow her head,
even when the lusting louse
wrenches her ever down.

You sheath your carnality in my shame,
and I wear it for you like a second skin.
The Ouroboros coils tighter.
This cycle, endless—
in it, one finds amnesty.
And one is left undone.

Inductee, abductee,
casualty of some ecclesiastical dream.
What was I meant to be?

Once, a woman.
Now, a pawn—
a piece in your fictional parson's
imaginary game of chess.

Rules that bind me,
moves I didn't choose.
All within the cloister of
your conclave's dominion.

12. (Wasted) Teeange Dream

How do I forget you?
I never could, nor ever will.
Yet here I must regret you.
In void you've left, the shame to fill.

Pressing for permission
My question lingered in your air.
Should I have stopped myself?
I guess we didn't care.

The world long saw
Depths of dark
Shattered nerves
Thoughts, long unorganized
Fears, snowball to avalanche

I hate you
I hate her
for making me
hate me.

And here now is a new me - a she.
She lives in a costume.
She exists under a new description.

Her character didn't play well
(with others, or in Peoria)
But the wretched crone still yet persists,
Marked with the scarlet stains
Left of your soft lips upon my soul
That scarlet slut I am
The bruises of her fingers
Wrapped around my heart

The saccharine kindness she dictated you feed me
Your translucent defense of the act of poisoning

A woman who wanted
To love you.

There was no world in which I met you
Only to not love you
There was no space and no time
In which I could not love you.

My words are whisperings as she screams.
My wants were nothing to you.

You are still
just a boy.
I am just like
other girls.

13. Senza Misura

Charmed out of my unbuttoned blouse
By your wit, your laugh, your sigh.
Pulling at seams just to pull –
You unravelled my fragile life.

Softly treading in your shadows,
Beneath the screaming, wailing sky,
Soon your laugh was just a dagger,
That threatened my shivering thigh.

Charmed out of my first-date dress,
Stole my buttons, left me on display.
As I yearned, I cried - I'd die to change!
Why – no – how could you be this way?

I had painted you with burning colors,
You only see my greys.
Your brown-eye, soulful, lover boy eyes –
For me, they've slipped away.

I wandered through the ruins,
Of this "us" I thought I saw.
Wasted tears still taint my sight.
My cold heart, left out to thaw.

In the atomic aftermath of the laughter,
The scars of your scorn and your sighs,
A bittersweet reminder,
Of the wreckage still inside.

Charmed away from myself, again.
One day, will I reclaim
The beauty from before the broken,
My strength beyond your shame.

14. Impersistence

Do I possess inherent value –
Or am I but inherent vice?

My soul belongs to the highest bidder –
Truly...at what price, soul?

Burdened to be of Christ's own vintage –
Can I sell that not under my ownership?

Should I deserve the ownership –
Should any of us seek to own our soul?

A penny, a pen, some Pyrex wares –
The crust of the bread of the wanted.

The touch or look or breath of a lover –
I am eager to sell for any hint of a smile.

The very essence of one's soul –
Is it love and be loved, or breath and dust to be dusted?

Seeking to return to the mud –
Perhaps a sale makes haste of time.

Is anyone seeking a soul to own –
Run down sole, worn for escape.

Could God spare a sinner's soul –
Even if he wanted to, why?

For what purpose does my soul remain –
Does it keep my heart flush with blood?

To what end, soul –
I cannot clean your spots and stains.

What, ho, soul –
Look upon the future I offer.

I beg for the purchase of this soul –
We do not belong to one another.

I am an empty vessel –
Take the bouquet to the bride.
She's just a tainted, tinted soul –
They've just been along for the ride.

15. What Was It Like for You?

I'd long said I only drink a sweet rosé,
And on that first, you still brought cabernet.
My heart was bruised; my knees still weakened, swayed.

Small, small, small—what's the use in being today?
When all you do is take, and I took, and I still take.
I'd long said I only drink a sweet rosé.

It's like my fate is just to make them pay—
Suffer at the discord I create and forsake.
My heart was bruised; my knees still weakened, swayed.

I'd rather be lone, living at the wake,
Than give my mind's irate dive or break.
I'd long said I only drink a sweet rosé.

Should I go, let me go—no farewell to make.
An escape was taken, protection for your sake.
My heart was bruised; my knees still weakened, swayed.

Say not goodbye; I leave no fruit to take.
This life of ours was far too short to stay.
I'd long said I only drink a sweet rosé—
My heart was bruised; my knees still weakened, swayed.

16. Finally, a Rest

You love me in such a way,
With a tongue for this foreign one I've not yet heard.
Intrinsic to you,
A smile that betrays love—
A love that I return.

I have seen the dark,
But in your arms, I find my light.
In a world where you are not,
There, I find my rest.
Your presence calls me home,
Whispering comfort in the quiet of the night.

The rhythm of your heart
Is the only drum I march to.
In its steady beat, I find my peace,
A melody woven through the warmth of your touch,
A dance we never learned but knew.

With you, there is no fear, no storm,
Only the warmth of your embrace.
In your heartbeat, I find my calm,
Guiding me through the world with grace.

17. Pash Rash - Act 1

X. The Prologue
Stitches embedded in fingers—
such is the story
of the bruise of a love that lingers.
A shade of burning red stains my skin,
tattooed by your callous scoff—
at the nonsense language
of heartbeats within.
You were never safe,
just familiar.

I. The Question
Have you found out what you wanted me for just yet?
I am a part for you to use in your play,
A melodic plot device—and I guess that's okay.
At least with me, I think I'm good.
You sort of treat me like you should.
Every morning, you wake up to her.
I never fell asleep.
Looking past the moody, muddy pools,
I found what you didn't see.
I know what you are to me.
But figure—
What am I in you?

II. The Push and Pull
I bounce back when you insult me and make me small.
I swing back into you when you spin me away.
You broke my gifts and gifted me nothing.
But still, your gift is being present.
Breathing in the dark,
The clean scent of hair too smooth
Between my fingers to be so undeservedly mine—
I snap back and remember it isn't.
It wasn't then.
Say it could have been.

III. The Self-Realization

I can honestly say I think I am what you need.
Maybe you're what I deserve.
I never said hello so I'd never have to say goodbye.
Now, every time you look at me—
In the before,
In the ask,
In the yes,
In the grip,
At the end,
Before I breathe again—
I say hi. Hey. Hello.
A thousand greetings to mitigate the feeling
Of the silent departure—
A bloody Irish Goodbye.

18. Pash Rash - Act 2

IV. The Inevitable Comparison
But his preference is redheads anyway.
I wasn't his type until I changed
My favorite things about myself.
Where am I in him?
I see what he is to me
And what I seem to be to him.
Every breath of mine he steals
Emboldens his love for everything I am not.
Shortens my time.
I am hopeless,
And he is as helpless.

V. The Distance
Less am I helpless,
And more do I find in him—
My self-destructive opportunism.
It reemerges
To see if I can lick the edge of the knife
You use to maintain the needed distance
Between me
And your respect,
Your love,
And anyone who looks, sounds, cries, asks, begs,
screams,
And breaks like I do.
There's nothing I hate more than
The way I am after you.

VI. The Heart's Humor
Your heart must have a sense of humor—
The way I watch your absent-minded,
Accidental comparisons.
Little things I do differently.
Little things she does so right.
Let me down gently.

My head is already at the base.
I await the way
My head is lopped
From the heart
That's beating in time
With the new kind of rhythm
I learned to dance to—
Just to keep in step with you.

VII. The Masquerade
The elevator music hums to your mind
(In those places where you sing to mine).
It's canned, it's panned,
Like late-night talk shows
When I'm in my masque,
Staying awake with my Ouija board,
Late-night TV with my demons
and some Devil
with his legions.

19. All the Space Between

He tells me he loves me
by standing between me and the cold.
But he won't say it, not a word.
His love is something unsaid,
something only I can feel.

Still, it's there—
in the way his lips brush mine,
in the way he draws me near
but never fully lets me in.
He thinks I don't see it,
thinks I'm too lost in what I want
to notice what I'm not getting.

I feel like I'm drifting away,
watching him try to love me.
I've watched myself
try to love who I am,
but there's always a part of me absent—
a fragment lost that I can't seem to fill.

He stands between me and the cold,
but never in the way of the silence
that settles in the space between us.

I'm not sure I'm loving him
or just loving the idea
of being loved,
of craving to fill the hollow
with anything I can find.

But still, I stay.
Not for the safety—
but for the comfort I know.

Maybe all I am is this—

a heart scarred from waiting,
a heart learning
to love myself
before I can ask for anything more.

20. In the Ether

In bated breath, I waited for the sound,
The words unspoken hung in disbelief,
Suspended where the silver pools are found.

I asked, but no firm answer could rebound,
Just whispered *I don't know,* so faint, so brief,
In bated breath, I waited for the sound.

To memories untainted, I was bound,
A fragile solace tempered by my grief,
Suspended where the silver pools are found.

Old wounds I pressed, their sharpness now profound,
Each ache a poignant rush, a strange relief,
In bated breath, I waited for the sound.

With senses wide, I tread this hollow ground,
The pain and wonder laced in bright motif,
Suspended where the silver pools are found.

Through haze of truth, the weight of loss astounds,
Yet still I walk, embraced by disbelief.
In bated breath, I waited for the sound,
Suspended where the silver pools are found.

21. San Andreas

I held your hand in the theater,
and it felt like holding a fault line,
the weight of everything unsaid
pressing between us.

When your breath broke,
your fist followed,
and I squeezed tighter,
as if I could stop the shaking,
as if my touch
could stitch you back together.

But I knew, even then—
your story had already ended.
Mine kept bleeding through blank pages,
the ink spelling your name
in lines I shouldn't still be writing.

Why does it hurt?
Because you'll never need me
the way I ache for you?
Or because, even if you did,
I would tear you apart?

And now I sit in the aftermath—
everyone I've loved turning cold,
truth cutting through me like static,
and still, it's you.
Always you.
And every moment since.